Stop, Pop!

by Marie Powell

illustrated by Amy Cartwright

Say Hello to Amicus Readers.

You'll find our helpful dog, Amicus, chasing a ball—to let you know the reading level of a book.

1

Learn to Read

Frequent repetition, high frequency words, and close photo-text matches introduce familiar topics and provide ample support for brand new readers.

2

Read Independently

Some repetition is mixed with varied sentence structures and a select amount of new vocabulary words are introduced with text and photo support.

3

Read to Know More

Interesting facts and engaging art and photos give fluent readers fun books both for reading practice and to learn about new topics.

Amicus Readers are published by Amicus
P.O. Box 1329, Mankato, MN 56002
www.amicuspublishing.us

Illustrations by Amy Cartwright

Produced for Amicus by The Peterson Publishing Company and Red Line Editorial.

Editor Jenna Gleisner
Designer Craig Hinton
Printed in the United States of America
North Mankato, MN
10 9 8 7 6 5 4 3 2 1

Library of Congress Cataloging-in-Publication Data

Powell, Marie, 1958- author.
 Stop, pop! / by Marie Powell ; illustrated by Amy Cartwright.
  pages cm. -- (Word Families)
 Summary: "Young readers meet a young girl and her Pop, who is always in a hurry, while learning words in the -op word family."
 Audience: K to Grade 3.
 ISBN 978-1-60753-925-4 (hardcover) --
 ISBN 978-1-68151-049-1 (pdf ebook)
 1. English language--Phonetics--Juvenile literature. 2. Vocabulary--Juvenile literature. 3. Reading--Phonetic method. 4. Readers (Primary) I. Cartwright, Amy, illustrator. II. Title.
 PE1135.P665 2016
 428'.1--dc23
                                        2015033471

Pop is always in a hurry.

"Hop out of bed!" he says.

"We're going to be late!"

Pop hurries to make eggs.
Flop! One by one they
drop to the floor.

I **mop** up the **slop**.

"Time to go!" says Pop.

"**Stop, Pop!** I need lunch,"
I say.

Pop starts to **chop** vegetables. Carrots and celery sticks cover the **countertop**.

"Hop to it! We still need to stop at the bookshop before school," says Pop.

I feel a raindrop on top of my head. Pop runs back for my coat.

Before I even **plop** my
backpack onto my back,
Pop drives off.
"**Stop**, **Pop**! You forgot
me!" I shout.

Word Family: -op

Word families are groups of words that rhyme and are spelled the same.

Here are the -op words in this book:

bookshop	plop
chop	Pop
countertop	raindrop
drop	slop
flop	stop
hop	top
mop	

Can you spell any other words with -op?